GOODB
2021
HELLO
2022

A reflective journal

With special thanks to our wonderful publisher Pavilion – to Kom, Cara and Helen for believing in our vision and being an all-round dream to work with. Thank you to our brilliant agent Valeria Huerta and to Fonz, Pav and Sammy for always being on this journey with us.

And a big thank you to our Project Love community for being a constant source of love and inspiration. We love you!

With all our love,

x Selina & Vicki

First published in the United Kingdom in 2021 by
Pavilion
43 Great Ormond Street
London
WC1N 3HZ

ISBN: 978-1-91168-215-8

A CIP catalogue record for this book is available from the British Library.

10 9 8 7 6 5 4 3 2 1

Reproduction by Rival Colour Ltd, UK
Printed and bound by Toppan Leefung Printing Ltd, China

www.pavilionbooks.com

GOODBYE 2021 HELLO 2022

A reflective journal

Project Love | PAVILION

"

OUR SOULS NEED TIME TO THINK, DREAM AND REFLECT.

JO ANN DAVIS

"

GOODBYE 2021, HELLO 2022

As one year comes to an end and another begins, it's time for you to take a step back. To pause for a moment in the rush of life. And reflect.

On the year that you've just been through. And the year that lies ahead.

And what a year it has been, as we continued to navigate life amidst a global pandemic and all of the fears, limitations and uncertainty that came with it.

In this journal, we invite you to reflect on what that experience was like for you – from the challenges and the setbacks to the gratitudes and the lessons that you learned along the way.

And then it's time to close the chapter on 2021 and to turn your focus to the year that lies ahead.

To get clear on what you'd love to make happen and how you'd love to feel in this brand new year and the dreams and goals that you'd love to bring to life.

So let's do that.

Let's say thank you and goodbye to 2021 as it comes to an end.

And get ready to fill 2022 with the things we love!

HOW THIS JOURNAL WORKS

Goodbye 2021, Hello 2022 guides you through a journey that helps you say a proper farewell to 2021, as it comes to an end, and create a vision and a plan for you to thrive and live a life you love in the year to come.

You'll begin by reflecting on all that has happened in your life in 2021 – your happiest moments, your achievements, the challenges you've overcome and the people you're grateful for. Then, through a series of questions and exercises, you'll be encouraged to think about what you need in life to feel happy, fulfilled and full of love. You'll use those ingredients to choose what you'd most like to focus on in 2022 and which dreams you'd like to bring to life.

By the end of the book, you will have in your hands a vision of the life you want to live in 2022, the dreams you want realized and a simple plan for how you're going to make it all happen.

Goodbye 2021, Hello 2022 will become your motivational journal for designing a life you love in 2022, with quarterly check-ins to help you keep on track throughout the year.

Remember, there is no right or wrong way to answer any of the questions in this book. Relax, have fun with it and just see what answers emerge on the page.

Don't worry if, with some questions, you draw a blank – you can always come back to them later or skip them all together. Not every question will be relevant to you this year.

For every question, you'll find you have a box to fill in with your answer. If you think that you need more space, there are some extra blank pages at the back of the book.

We have loved seeing what *Goodbye, Hello* has done for people over the past nine years and now we can't wait to see what it will do for you!

SHARE WITH US!

There is nothing we love more than seeing photos of you using your *Goodbye, Hello* journals. It is so exciting to see people all over the world dreaming and designing their lives into the pages of this book and sharing their experiences with us.

Share a photo of you doing your *Goodbye, Hello* journal with us:

ⓞ @loveprojectlove

#thegoodbyehellojournal

✉ hello@loveprojectlove.com

And look what we've made for you!

A free audio tutorial on '*How to turn your dreams into reality in 2022*'

Come and get it over at
www.thegoodbyehellojournal.com/dreams

x Selina & Vicki

"

AS WE REFLECT
WE CONNECT
WITH OUR
DEEPEST SELVES
AND REMEMBER
HOW PRECIOUS
THIS LIFE OF
OURS IS.

"

GOODBYE 2021

A lot can change,

a lot can happen

in just <u>one</u> year.

Let's see what's

<u>happened</u> in

your life...

WHAT HAPPENED IN YOUR LIFE IN 2021?

Here we are at the end of another year. A year which began amidst a global pandemic that continued to turn our worlds upside down, but which (we hope) is ending with us being able to see and hug our loved ones and start to look to a future free of COVID-19 and life in lockdown.

It's been a rollercoaster year and, in amongst it all, each of us will have had our own ups and downs – happy times as well as hard times. We will all have grown, learnt important lessons and made things happen in our lives.

So let's now reflect on how the year has been *for you*.

If, at first, you find it hard to recall things, then take it slowly. Go month by month, perhaps using your calendar to help remind you of what you got up to over the past year.

Remember that there are no right or wrong answers to any of these questions. You might have just a few lines to write for one question, but with others, you might have so much you want to write that you'll need to use the extra pages at the back of the book.

And don't be hard on yourself if there were dreams and plans you had at the start of 2021 that didn't happen. A lot of dreams have had to be put on hold over the past two years so that we could focus on looking after ourselves and those we love as we got through the pandemic.

Getting through it has been an achievement enough!

The key in answering these questions is to relax, spend a little time pondering each question and enjoy this process of reflecting and spending quality time with yourself.

11

"

WHEN YOU WRITE YOUR STORY, LESSONS EMERGE THAT YOUR SOUL WISHES YOU TO SEE.

"

What was going on in your life this time last year?

How were you feeling?

As you looked ahead to 2021, what did you want it to be all about for you?

What happened in 2021?

What were the main events and milestones in your life in 2021?

What did you create, achieve and make happen in 2021 (the big and the small)?

WHAT WERE THE MAIN EVENTS AND MILESTONES IN YOUR LIFE IN 2021?

What were your happiest moments?

When did you have the most fun?

When and where did you feel the most at peace?

What has been the most unexpected thing about this year?

What new thing(s) did you discover about yourself?

When did you feel the most love?

What are you particularly proud of?

What have been your hardest moments in 2021?

What have been your biggest challenges?

What are the most important lessons you have learned?

What will 2021 be remembered for in your life?

GRATITUDE

GRATITUDE IS HAPPINESS DOUBLED BY WONDER.

G. K. CHESTERTON

THE POWER OF GRATITUDE

Gratitude is the simple but powerful practice of expressing thanks and giving appreciation for what you have in your life, right now.

Research shows that the practice of gratitude improves your health, increases your happiness and productivity and helps you to foster deep and fulfilling relationships.

At Project Love, we also believe it is a key tool when it comes to designing a life you love, because whatever you focus your attention on, you get more of. Thinking about what you are grateful for, rather than envying what you are lacking, helps to keep you in a positive mindset and the life you dream of feels perfectly possible. Your actions and choices then align with that dream life, help invite it in and make it happen.

Let's create more of what you want in life by taking some time to reflect on all that you're grateful for having in your life right now...

At the moment, what are you grateful for in your life?

Who are you grateful for?

What about yourself are you grateful for this year?

"

TRUE HAPPINESS IS ALWAYS AVAILABLE TO US, BUT FIRST WE HAVE TO CREATE THE ENVIRONMENT FOR IT TO FLOURISH.

SAKYONG MIPHAM RINPOCHE

"

WHAT DO YOU WANT TO FILL YOUR LIFE WITH?

Now that you've said a proper farewell to 2021, it's time to turn your attention towards 2022. Look at the fresh new canvas ahead of you and choose what you want to fill it with.

In order for you to be able to do that, you first need to be clear on what it is you need in life to feel happy, alive, fulfilled and full of love – this year and beyond. And that is what this next section is all about.

Over the following pages, you're going to build up a juicy list of all the things that make you happy in life: the things you love to do, the people you love to spend your time with and the places you love to spend your time in.

You're going to look back to some of your happiest times in life and the ingredients that helped to make you so happy then and you're going to allow yourself to imagine what you would love your dream life to look like five years from now.

Now we know that, since COVID arrived in our lives, a lot of the things we loved to do were taken off the menu and many dreams had to be put on hold and we hope that by the time you are writing in this journal, most limitations will have been lifted. However, if you are still unable to do some of the things that make you come alive and bring you joy, still include them over the following pages. Include all the ingredients that make you happy in life, even if some are still not possible for now.

As in the previous section, there are no right or wrong answers to any of these questions. You might have loads to write for one and just a sentence to write on the next. And don't be surprised if you find yourself repeating some answers – this just helps to highlight what is particularly important to you at the moment.

So relax your mind, let your imagination go and see what emerges on the page in front of you as you start to write...

HELLO YOU

"

AT THE CENTRE OF YOUR BEING, YOU HAVE THE ANSWER; YOU KNOW WHO YOU ARE AND YOU KNOW WHAT YOU WANT.

LAO TZU

"

What makes you feel happy, alive and fulfilled in life?

WHAT ARE THE THINGS YOU LOVE TO DO?

What simple pleasures do you enjoy?

What activities make you come alive?

What activities help you to feel calm and relaxed?

What do you love to do on your time off or at weekends?

What do you love to do on holiday?

What are the things that you could spend all day doing and never get tired of?

What activities do you love to do with the people you love?

What activities do you love to do on your own?

Think back to your happiest moments in life – what were you doing that made you so happy?

WHERE ARE THE PLACES YOU LOVE TO SPEND TIME IN?

Where do you feel your happiest? (This can be a specific place, such as at home, or a more general area – by the sea, for example.)

What places (or kinds of places) do you feel most at peace and relaxed in?

Where are the places that you have the most fun?

What are the kinds of places you like to visit on holiday?

What places in the world would you one day love to visit?

Think back to your happiest moments in life – where were you that made you so happy?

WHO ARE THE PEOPLE YOU LOVE TO BE WITH?

Who are the people that make you happy in life?

Who are the people you feel most loved by?

Who are the people that inspire you most in life? (You can include people you know, people you follow online or even fictional or historical characters.)

Who are the people you feel you can be most yourself with? And why?

Who are the people that really see your value?

HOW DO YOU LOVE TO FEEL?

When you're at your happiest at home, how do you feel?

When you're at your happiest at work, how do you feel?

When you're at your happiest on your own, how do you feel?

When you're at your happiest among people, how do you feel?

HOW DO YOU LIKE TO LOOK
AFTER YOURSELF?

What helps you to feel good in your body and mind? E.g. plenty of water, exercise, eight hours of sleep, yoga, meditation etc...

What helps to recharge your batteries when you've tired yourself out?

What life do you dream of?

TAKE YOUR DREAMS SERIOUSLY

Our ability to dream and then make those dreams happen is the magic we have as human beings.

It is what gives us the power to be able to bring about change in our own lives and in the world around us, and it is therefore a key tool when it comes to designing a life you truly love.

So, over the following few pages, you're going to allow yourself to dream – and dream BIG.

Let yourself imagine that anything is possible and see what dreams emerge when you allow yourself to do that...

DREAMS COME TRUE. WITHOUT THAT POSSIBILITY, NATURE WOULD NOT INCITE US TO HAVE THEM.

JOHN UPDIKE

YOUR DREAM LIFE

The key to dreaming and dreaming BIG is to give yourself permission – permission to imagine that anything is possible and to dream from there.

So let's imagine you have a magic wand that you can use to conjure up whatever you want in your own life: your dream home, dream career, dream relationship – whatever it is you want, you can have it.

Now imagine that you're living that life five years from now.

Take yourself there for a moment and describe what that life is like. And don't hold back. Let yourself dream as wildly as your imagination allows...

Where do you live?

What is your home like?

How do you spend your days?

What do you do on your time off?

What kind of holidays do you go on?

Who are the special people in your life?

What have you achieved over the past five years?
(Remember that this is five years into the future.)

Is there anything else you can see in this dream life of yours?

How does it feel to live this life?

What is it that you love the MOST about this life of yours?

DREAMS ARE ILLUSTRATIONS... FROM THE BOOK YOUR SOUL IS WRITING ABOUT YOU.

MARSHA NORMAN

As you look at your 'dream life', which parts do you want to start introducing the most in 2022?

What practical steps can you take to get started on bringing those dreams to life in 2022?

HELLO
2022

"

YOUR LIFE
IS ONE BIG
CANVAS. AND
YOU ARE THE
ARTIST. PAINT
IT WITH THE
THINGS YOU
LOVE.

"

HELLO 2022

Stepping into a fresh new year is like starting a new chapter in a book. But in this book, you are the one that is writing the story. You get to choose what you fill the pages with, what direction the story goes in and what dreams get brought to life.

So...what do you want this next chapter in your life to be all about? What do you want to fill your life with in 2022? What do you want to make happen? What do you want to experience? How do you want to feel?

It's time to choose.

Creating a life you love is about listening to your dreams, your needs and your desires and then choosing which ones you want to focus on bringing into your life.

As you look back at your answers in this journal so far, it's time to see which dreams are calling to you the most, which ingredients you most want to fill this year with and what you want to choose as your 2022 focus.

Over the following pages, you'll be asked questions designed to help you get clear on what you want to make your 2022 all about.

Don't worry if you don't have an answer to every question. Just answer the ones that speak to you.

As with every other section, you will likely find that there are some questions you have clear answers for, while others don't feel so relevant to you this year.

And there may still be some things currently off the menu due to COVID. If that is the case and it is messing with your ability to dream freely, consider that those dreams are simply on pause. There will be other years when those dreams can be brought back into play. For now, focus on what is available to you and use those ingredients to create a life you love in 2022, no matter what is going on in the world around you.

So let's turn the page and start designing your 2022...

WHAT DO YOU WANT TO MAKE YOUR 2022 ALL ABOUT?

Which of your dreams do you want to bring to life this year (or start to bring to life)?

What changes (if any) do you want to make in your life in 2022?

What challenges do you want to take on (if any) in 2022?

How do you want to see yourself grow in 2022?

What else do you want to do or make happen in 2022?

What else do you want your life to be full of (people, places, activities, holidays, experiences...)?

WHAT DO YOU WANT TO FEEL IN 2022?

Look back at your answers on how you love to feel on page 38 and circle, below, the feelings that call out to you and add any of your own...

calm • joy • fun • peace • happiness • love

inspiration • connection • focus • playfulness

power • contentment • fulfillment • nourishment

vitality • abundance • freedom • gratitude • ease

serenity • courage • passion • stillness • strength

softness • integrity • lightness • celebration

generosity • balance • kindness • wonder

commitment • optimism • unity • purpose

clarity • compassion...

Now choose one to three feelings that you most
want to experience in 2022

In 2022 I want to feel...

What do you want to make your 2022 all about?

THE POWER OF CHOOSING A FOCUS FOR YOUR YEAR

OK, now we are getting to the big moment in your *Goodbye, Hello* journey: it's time for you to choose your focus for the new year.

What do you want to make 2022 all about? What do you want your focus to be?

Having a focus for your year acts like a guiding star, helping to guide your choices and actions in the direction of your dreams.

It is a way for you to commit seriously; to yourself, to your happiness and wellbeing and to creating a life you love.

Over the following pages, you'll find guidance on how to choose your focus, but ultimately it is about choosing a focus that makes you feel good when you imagine a whole year of making that a priority.

So, have a read through of the different ways you can choose your focus, look back over the previous pages in this section and choose a focus that really makes you smile.

DREAMS AND DEDICATION ARE A POWERFUL COMBINATION.

WILLIAM LONGGOOD

HOW TO CHOOSE YOUR FOCUS

The most important thing is that you choose a focus that feels good for you. Never choose a focus for your year because you think you should or because you think it sounds good. Choose a focus for your year that gets you feeling excited and looking forward to the year that lies ahead.

Here are a few different ways you can choose your focus for the year:

Option 1: Choose something that you want more of in your life.

You might be craving more of something in your life like...

Creativity, fun, love, calm, adventure, celebration, nourishment, laughter, peace, clarity, gratitude, self-care, connection, femininity, vitality, self-love, magic.

And so you could make that your focus for 2022 and commit to cultivating more of that into your life in the year to come:

'2022 is my year of fun.'
'2022 is my year of creativity.'
'2022 is my year of self-care.'

Option 2: Choose an intention for the year.

Maybe, as you've been answering the questions in your journal so far, you've felt a desire to set an intention for this year. You might not know how it's going to manifest, but that is part of the magic of it: you set the intention and see how it grows. You just know that this is what you want to make this year all about:

'2022 is my year of stepping into my power.'
'2022 is my year of standing in love.'
'2022 is my year of designing a life I love.'
'2022 is my year of healing.'
'2022 is my year of saying "yes!"'

Option 3: Choose a big change you want to make or a big dream you want to bring to life.

Maybe this is the year when you really feel ready to commit and make that big change happen, or bring that big dream to life. And so that is what you want to choose as your 2022 focus to really fire up your commitment and make it your central focus for the year:

'2022 is my year of starting my own business.'
'2022 is my year of finding an exciting new career path.'
'2022 is my year of buying my first home.'
'2022 is my year of creating my home in a new country.'
'2022 is my year of taking a six-month sabbatical.'

That said, even if you do have a big change you want to make or big dream you want to bring to life in 2022, you don't have to choose that as your focus. You might prefer to focus on how you want to approach making that change. For example, you might want 2022 to be the year that you really get your career change going, but rather than making 2022 your year of 'career change', you might choose to make it your year of 'self-care', to help you focus on looking after your wellbeing while you go through a big life change.

Option 4: Just go with what your gut says.

If you just *know* what you want your focus for 2022 to be, even if it doesn't fit into Options 1 to 3, then go for it. The key with choosing your focus is that it is meaningful and inspiring to *you*.

Now it's time for you to choose a focus for your 2022...

2022

is my year of

. . . .

Why do you want that to be your focus for 2022?

So let's make it happen!

HOW TO DESIGN A LIFE
YOU LOVE IN 2022

Designing a life you love doesn't happen by accident. Whatever your dreams, your desires, your visions for this year and the future, it isn't luck that will make them happen. It is you taking action that will ultimately have you creating a life you love.

So now it's time to come up with as many things as you can think of that will help you make 2022 your year of:

. . . .

You can choose big things and small things.

For example, if you chose 2022 to be your year of 'adventure', then maybe there are a few big adventures you know you want to go on in 2022 or that you already have booked in. Write those down. But don't stop there. What other things could you do to bring adventure into your life this year, even in small ways? Really have some fun with this and, if you struggle to come up with ideas, ask a friend to help brainstorm ideas with you.

On the next page, write down at least 10 things you could do this year to bring your dreams and intentions to life. And do come back to this list and add things to it, as and when you think of them.

All the things I could do, big or small, to make 2022 my year of.....:

"

THERE CAME A TIME WHEN THE RISK TO REMAIN TIGHT IN THE BUD WAS MORE PAINFUL THAN THE RISK IT TOOK TO BLOSSOM.

ANAÏS NIN

"

CHOOSE THREE THINGS TO FOCUS ON FIRST...

Now it's time to commit to doing THREE THINGS between now and April that are aligned with your focus for 2022 and/or support you in creating a life you love.

We have found over the years that three is the magic number when it comes to making commitments, because it keeps them memorable and manageable and therefore far more likely to succeed.

When it comes to choosing your commitments, there are three simple rules:

1. They have to be aligned with your focus for 2022, support you in creating a life you love or simply make you *feel* good.

2. They have to be something you *want* to do and not something you feel you *should* do.

3. They have to be specific – if one of your commitments, for example, is to learn to cook then don't just write down 'I'm going to learn to cook'. Get specific about how, where, when and how often. E.g. 'I'm going to learn to cook one new dish each week' or 'I'm going to sign up to cooking classes and do them every Thursday night'.

And then open up your calendar and schedule in the first step you're going to take to get that commitment going (for example, 'research cooking books and courses').

WHAT I WILL DO
JANUARY – MARCH 2022

The three things I commit to doing between now and 31 March:

1.

2.

3.

DECLARE IT

Now that you have your focus for 2022 and your commitments between now and April set, it is time for the final step: to declare your focus and commitments to the world.

Because it is when you start sharing with others what your game plan is for 2022 that the magic really begins. Opportunities start to appear, things seem to align themselves and you'll suddenly begin to notice paths towards your dreams that you might never have thought of before.

So it is time to declare your focus for 2022 to someone in your life. Someone who counts. Someone who loves and supports you and wants to see you live a life you love.

Who will that person be?

. . . .

Let them know what you are committing to doing in 2022 and ask that they hold you to account.

"TAKE THE FIRST STEP IN FAITH, YOU DON'T HAVE TO SEE THE WHOLE STAIRCASE, JUST TAKE THE FIRST STEP.

MARTIN LUTHER KING

A MESSAGE FROM YOU TO YOU

Learning to give yourself the words of encouragement and support that help you to move forwards is every bit as important as creating a plan and taking action when you are creating a life you love.

However, most of us tend to be our own harshest critics and we are more tuned into the negative, critical side of ourselves that is ready to point out where we're failing and cast doubt over whether we really have what it takes to make our dreams happen. We often only use our loving, supportive side on our loved ones. Now it's time to turn that loving attention towards yourself.

Let that side of you write a message of encouragement to you as you step into 2022, ready to make you and your happiness a top priority and ready to create a life you love...

My message from me to me...

And so the journey begins...

"THE MAGIC WE HAVE AS HUMAN BEINGS IS OUR ABILITY TO DREAM THINGS UP AND THEN MAKE THEM HAPPEN. GO AND USE YOUR MAGIC!"

DESIGNING A LIFE YOU LOVE IN 2022

DESIGNING A LIFE YOU LOVE IN 2022

One of the main problems with our traditional New Year's resolutions is that we create a list of the things we'd like to achieve over the course of the year, get excited about it and then, by the time we've hit February, we're so caught up in the rush of life that our sparkly list of New Year's resolutions has been pretty much forgotten.

According to research, only 8 per cent of New Year's resolutions ever happen and 50 per cent fail within the first month.

So, with *Goodbye, Hello* we do things differently.

We get you to hold onto just one main focus for the year and then commit to doing just three things every three months that will help you to stick to your focus for 2022 and design a life you love.

At the start of every quarter (that is, the start of April, July and October) we bring you back to your *Goodbye, Hello* journal so that you can check in with yourself, reflect on the previous three months and revisit your three commitments to see how you got on.

You then set three fresh new commitments for the following three months; commitments that support you in creating a life that you love.

Come and follow us over on Instagram and we'll remind you at the start of each quarter when it's time for your quarterly check-in.

@loveprojectlove

Living a life you love doesn't happen by accident. It isn't down to luck. It's down to you.

Remind yourself of your dreams on a regular basis and keep taking practical steps until you've made those dreams come true.

QUARTERLY CHECK-INS

YOU ARE EXACTLY WHERE YOU NEED TO BE.

@MEESHNAH

APRIL

APRIL REFLECTIONS

It's time to take a step back and review how things have been going over the past three months. What have you been up to? Have you been making time in your life for the things that are most important to you? Have you been doing things to bring to life your focus for 2022? How did you get on with your three commitments? Let's take a look... and if you want to do your review together with us then tune into the Project Love podcast.

How are you feeling at the moment?

What has happened in your life since January?

What have you done that you're proud of?

What have been your happiest moments?

What have been your most challenging moments?

What and who are you grateful for at this moment in your life?

APRIL CHECK-IN

Go and take a look at your focus for 2022 and the three things you committed to doing. It's time to review how things have been going:

What have you done from that list of commitments?

What haven't you done from that list of commitments?

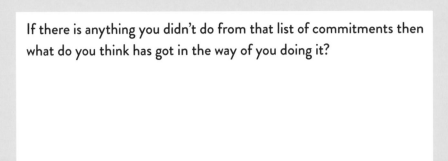

If there is anything you didn't do from that list of commitments then what do you think has got in the way of you doing it?

Do you want to carry this commitment through to the next quarter? If you do, then what can you do to make sure you prioritize it between now and 30 June?

Take a moment to remind yourself of your focus for 2022 and return to the list you made on page 66. What on that list appeals to you the most right now? Is there anything you want to add to it?

Now choose the THREE THINGS you most want to commit to doing over the next three months and write them down on the next page.

WHAT I WILL DO
APRIL – JUNE 2022

The three things I commit to doing between now and 30 June:

1.

2.

3.

"

WE HAVE TO EMBRACE OBSTACLES TO REACH THE NEXT STAGE OF JOY.

GOLDIE HAWN

"

JULY

JULY REFLECTIONS

It's time to take a step back and review how things have been going over the past three months. What have you been up to? Have you been making time in your life for the things that are most important to you? Have you been doing things to bring to life your focus for 2022? How did you get on with your three commitments? Let's take a look... and if you want to do your review together with us then tune into the Project Love podcast.

How are you feeling at the moment?

What has happened in your life since April?

What have you done that you're proud of?

What have been your happiest moments?

What have been your most challenging moments?

What and who are you grateful for at this moment in your life?

JULY CHECK-IN

Go and take a look at your focus for 2022 and the three practical steps you committed to taking between April and now. It's time to review how things have been going:

What have you done from that list of commitments?

What haven't you done from that list of commitments?

If there is anything you didn't do from that list of commitments, then what do you think has got in the way of you doing it?

Do you want to carry this commitment through to the next quarter? If you do, then what can you do to make sure you prioritize it between now and 30 September?

Take a moment to remind yourself of your focus for 2022 and return to the list you made on page 66. What on that list appeals to you the most right now? Is there anything you want to add to it?

Now choose the THREE THINGS you most want to commit to doing over the next three months and write them down on the next page.

WHAT I WILL DO
JULY – SEPTEMBER 2022

The three things I commit to doing between now and 30 September.

1.

2.

3.

YOU CAN WRITE A NEW STORY (OR EDIT YOUR CURRENT ONE) WHENEVER OR HOWEVER YOU WANT.

OCTOBER

OCTOBER REFLECTIONS

It's time to take a step back and review how things have been going over the past three months. What have you been up to? Have you been making time in your life for the things that are most important to you? Have you been doing things to bring to life your focus for 2022? How did you get on with your three commitments? Let's take a look... and if you want to do your review together with us then tune into the Project Love podcast.

How are you feeling at the moment?

What has happened in your life since July?

What have you done that you're proud of?

What have been your happiest moments?

What have been your most challenging moments?

What and who are you grateful for at this moment in your life?

OCTOBER CHECK-IN

Go and take a look at your focus for 2022 and the three practical steps you committed to taking between July and now. It's time to review how things have been going:

What have you done from that list of commitments?

What haven't you done from that list of commitments?

If there is anything you didn't do from that list of commitments, then what do you think has got in the way of you doing it?

Do you want to carry this commitment through to the next quarter? If you do, then what can you do to make sure you prioritize it between now and 31 December?

Take a moment to remind yourself of your focus for 2022 and return to the list you made on page 66. What on that list appeals to you the most right now? Is there anything you want to add to it?

Now choose the THREE THINGS you most want to commit to doing over the next three months and write them down on the next page.

WHAT I WILL DO
OCTOBER – DECEMBER 2022

The three things I commit to doing between now and 31 December:

1.

2.

3.

" "

IT IS NEVER TOO LATE TO BE WHAT YOU MIGHT HAVE BEEN.

GEORGE ELIOT

" "

TIME TO REFLECT ON 2022

A FINAL REFLECTION

And so we've come to the end of another year. It is time to take a step back and reflect on all that has happened in 2022 and, in particular, on which of the intentions and dreams written into the pages of this journal have become a reality in your life this past year.

Now, not all of those intentions and dreams will have materialized and that's OK. Some dream seeds grow and flourish and others don't.

For now, we want you to reflect on the dreams written into this journal that *did* come true in 2022 and how having a focus for your year helped you to flourish.

So let's start by taking a look at your focus for 2022.

2022 was my year of ....

What has it been like to have this as your focus for a year?

How did you help to make your 2022 about that?

Read through page 48 and pages 52–54 and write down the dreams you wanted to bring to life, the changes you wanted to make, how you wanted to grow and what you wanted to make happen in 2022.

Which of the things you wrote down *did* happen this year?

Is there anything you wrote down that didn't happen this year and you wish it had?

What can you do to help make that happen in 2023?

As you look back on 2022 and the dreams *you* brought to life and the intentions that shaped your year, take a moment to celebrate yourself. Celebrate your power to create your own reality and your ability to bring your dreams to life and to materialize the changes you wanted to see in your own life and the world around you.

How does it feel to know that you can be the artist of your own life and are taking steps, big and small, to create the life you want to be living?

GOODBYE FOR NOW

And so with that, your *Goodbye 2021, Hello 2022* journey is complete!

Forgive yourself if there were any dreams, intentions or commitments that you didn't bring to life this year. It's not about getting a perfect score (not at all!). Instead, focus on what you did create and make happen in your life. And celebrate!

Life design, at its core, is about recognizing that you have the power to be the artist of your own life. You possess the magic that all human beings have, of being able to make your dreams a reality.

All it takes is the willingness to allow yourself to dream, take those dreams seriously and turn them into projects and actions that, step by step, will bring those dreams to life.

So grab a hold of that magic that you possess and we'll see you over in the *Goodbye 2022, Hello 2023 journal* for another year of creating a life you love!

With all our love,

x Selina & Vicki

KEEP AN EYE ON **THEGOODBYEHELLOJOURNAL.COM**
TO LOOK FOR UPDATES ON THE NEXT GOODBYE, HELLO JOURNAL

NOTES

NOTES

NOTES

NOTES